First Steps

to helping couples prepare for marriage

Michael K. Lea, Ph.D.

ISBN-978-0-692-20910-3

Acknowledgements

Thank you to the many people who participated in bringing this book to fruition especially Rev. Loyce Craft and Rick Tancreto for their input.

To John and Lauren, Christopher and Jacqueline, and Seth and Cara thank you so much for agreeing to be test couples on the effectiveness of the following pages. Each of your marriages is a wonderful example of how great things are when God is first.

Table of Contents

Introduction

Almost immediately after releasing my last book entitled, <u>So You Think You Are Married ... Ten Tips On How To Live Like It.</u> (Westbow Press, 2011) I was approached by counselors, pastors, engaged couples, and singles on writing a book for those who are not married. My previous book was not appropriate for unmarried couples because the assignments created a level of intimacy that might place the couple in jeopardy of falling into sin.

It is important to emphasize that the approach to mentoring taken in this book is based on the biblical view of marriage i.e. a union between one man and one woman.

In my role as a pastor I have resisted performing a wedding ceremony for couples who did not wish to commit to between six to eight sessions of pre-marriage mentoring. Many engaged couples act so much in love that they are often unrealistic about what a successful and God-honoring marriage looks like. A lot of these couples have not taken the time to talk through the intricate dynamics of a marriage relationship. The role of the mentor, counselor, or pastor is to compel couples to ask the hard questions about relationship building, and to equip the couple with the right tools for success.

Pre-marriage mentoring does not guarantee the success of a marriage. The mentoring process allows the couple to talk openly and honestly about how to handle married life issues before they actually encounter that particular issue. When a couple encounters some difficulty they are then able to know that they have talked it through and have a committed plan to resolve things. The mentoring process is more effective at helping couples build on the strengths that already exist in their relationship. It is important for the couple providing the mentoring to be familiar with the many assessments available for strengthening couples.

An important part of helping couples with marriage preparation is the action item assignments each individual is given. The goal is to help each person learn to delight in who they are in the Lord, accept the call that God has on Christian marriages, and to protect their marriage from attacks outside of the marriage. As each person develops his or her individual insight, the couple is led through discussions that are meant to develop unity in the relationship. Unity, prior to being married, better promotes unity after the wedding vows are said. Most of us know that being married does not automatically bring about a unified understanding on important aspects of marriage life such as spiritual growth, finances, child rearing, life goals, or many other segments of the married life. It is not surprising to know that a couple not unified in the important things of marriage, or even in the everyday things of doing life prior to marriage, will have a very difficult time developing that unity after they are married.

If I could have a perfect world, I would have couples spend more time and money planning for the success of the relationship parts of the marriage than they spend on preparing for the wedding. To that end I am convinced that couples should pay for pre-marriage mentoring. The willingness to invest in the pre-marriage mentoring is an immediate indicator of how difficult a time a couple will have in the first few years, and even beyond. Even if a mentoring ministry does not charge for its services, the engaged couple or individual should understand there is an implied value to paying for the time spent, even if it is called a gift. Another learning benefit is to know that the Bible teaches us that the worker is due his pay. (Luke 10:7)

Marriage takes a plan to be a success. A successful marriage doesn't happen without a plan. A plan has to be discussed and agreed upon to realistically prevent from being surprised by the attacks that Satan sends at newlyweds. One of his most predominant attack methods is to entice engaged couples to cross the line in physical intimacy. When my wife and I enter into a mentoring relationship we state, as strongly as possible, that the physical nature of the pre-marriage relationship

x

must be pure. Satan's desire is that the engaged couple not strive for purity. If they can be moved to play at being married by living together, or being sexually intimate, then when they are actually married, a state of confusion develops. We admonish each couple to remain pure, or return to a state of purity, so God can be called upon to bless the upcoming marriage.

God ordained marriage with a plan from the time He first acknowledged that it was not good for man to be alone (Genesis 2:18). God created man and woman to complete and complement each other so that His plan for creation would be complete. Marriage is created beyond the need to provide companionship. The marriage relationship is necessary for the orderly propagation of the human race. God ordained marriage as the best way to raise and nurture children.

It should not surprise us that God's creation of marriage is constantly under attack. Satan desires that the very institution God created for the success of his creation would be destroyed at its core. Marriages must work hard to protect against such destruction. Pre-marriage mentoring is essential in helping couples prepare themselves to build a shield of understanding through prayer, study, and fellowship in the Christian community.

For many years, a large part of my ministry has been the working with engaged and married couples to enhance their marriage relationship. Mentoring provided to couples is performed with my wife. As a couple, we are able to address a multitude of needs that couples have in marriage. My wife brings a healthy and refreshing perspective to the discussion. Many times she will bring up a topic that is obvious to a woman, and yet eludes the man. I always learn something new when this happens. Another great benefit that we have experienced is that a couple mentoring a couple creates a safer environment for everyone. The arrangement removes the two men against a woman, or vice versa, that may develop and makes the discussions more comfortable.

The following pages represent the process that I have used with a multitude of couples over the last 15 years. Couples are encouraged to go through the chapters individually to examine their hearts and their preparedness for marriage. Each couple should work with a mentor couple to help them discuss their growth and expectations. In choosing a mentor couple, the engaged couple should choose a married couple that models the example of Christian living, and who will commit to walk alongside them for a full season of eight weeks. It may take less time, but it is important to have helpers who are willing to invest their all in such a life changing encounter. This mentor couple will likely be part of the couple's life from then on. At least, that is the experience I have had over the years. Ideally, the mentor couple would be a pastor, counselor, or trained lay leaders, who have been trained in communication and the use of assessments. In our ministry we have all the above. The ministry is actually led by an Elder and his wife who submitted to many hours of training. The passion they have to help couples be successful is contagious. An attribute that engaged couples should look for in finding a mentoring couple is passion. If you don't have access to a mentoring or pre-marriage ministry, do not be afraid to ask the hard questions of the people you desire to be part of your journey. The couple you ask will be blessed even if they can't commit to the time. Ask them to pray for you, and seek God's guidance for the couple He has prepared to be your mentors.

If the officiant for the wedding has been chosen, the engaged couple should seek counsel and prayer from that person in deciding on the mentoring couple. It is not unusual that the person who performs the wedding ceremony is not the person involved in the pre-marriage mentoring. This person would be instrumental in working with the mentoring couple to provide a time when the engaged could pray together without being alone.

Who Is First?

As you prepare for marriage the most important segment of your life that you should have in order is that of your prayer life, your time with God, your quiet time. So many people get so busy preparing for the wedding that they lose sight of the very thing that will provide them with stability in their marriage - their relationship with God. It is important to establish a foundation in your relationship that is centered on Christ. To be able to pray with your prospective spouse after the wedding about all the aspects of your married life is an integral part for success. It is often bewildering to me when I sit with pastors, elders, Christian leaders, and Christian couples and ask the question, "What is your prayer life like?" The answer I usually get is, "Well, it's not what it should be." That is a very distressing answer. Probably what makes it so distressing is that after some examination with a couple, I find it is not only not what it should be, it is nonexistent.

If there was ever a time that you should be really focused on your prayer life, it is this time in your life. In preparing to spend the rest of your life with the person God has placed in your life, you need to be covered in prayer. Be careful not to fall into the trap that makes prayer a mystical thing that's unattainable. For most of us, prayer is just a conversation with God. You might not always find yourself on your knees, in your bed, or in your prayer closet when you have a conversation with God. If you really start paying attention to it, you will probably realize that you pray more often than you know. It may be in your car when you think about your loved one and find yourself asking God to bless them. It may be just before a conversation about which band, which food, which hotel, which vacation, or which whatever, that you have during times of wedding planning. More than likely, you find yourself praying when you think about how blessed you are to have this man or woman in your life, to whom you will soon be married.

So don't let the topic of prayer be intimidating. Prayer is as easy as a conversation. It's even easier when the conversation is with someone you love, and who loves you. This conversation may be with God, or it may be with your future spouse. In either case, how can it be difficult?

Over the many years of working with couples, I've come to learn that wives desire to have their husband lead them, and pray over them. The wives know they could take over and recommend praying daily with their husband. However, deep inside they know this is not their spiritual responsibility. One thing you should know about prayer is that wives have told me that they often see prayer as more intimate than sex. At least, that's what the information I've been given seems to indicate. Some years ago I read a book by Larry Crabb entitled <u>The Silence of Adam.</u> I came away from reading Mr. Crabb's book realizing that each time that I chose not to pray with my wife I was behaving in much the same way when Adam watched Eve be deceived and did not intervene. Eve was not given the direction by God. Adam was.

Adam turned around and blamed God indicating it's the woman that God gave him who has caused the problems.

In reality, it is Adam's failure to act that caused the problem. Each time you decide not to pray over your spouse after you're married, in my mind, you are turning your marriage over to Satan. The act of not praying with your spouse only invites Satan into your marriage.

As you prepare for marriage it is important that you prepare your heart to be able to pray for your spouse. **(I do not recommend that an engaged couple pray together, or pray over each other.)** It is certainly all right to pray for each other, but what I've noticed is that Satan will take the time that you set aside to pray with each other, and over each other, and the intimacy that it provides, to make it something that's not of God. What I know is that Satan will try to trick you into believing that intimacy already exists so why not just cross some other line that he has attempted to blur. I think it's important for you to be encouraged by your mentoring couple to take the time to pray together while you're in their midst,

4

but your separate prayer lives should remain separate, until after the wedding.

For many years I would pray with my wife at the end of the day before we both went to sleep. We often found that we were so fatigued that we could barely get in a few sentences, much less hear from God, or each other about what our prayer needs were. Yet, we continued to pray in the evening as I thought this was at least obedient to God's calling for me to pray with my spouse. I understood clearly Matthew 18:20 that reads, "For where two or three come together in my name, there I am with them." I knew, and I hope that you know, that to pray in a disjointed fashion does not honor God. It is more about being in agreement with our loved one, and then seeking God's Will. Just as unity in the other areas of marriage is important, so it is even more important with prayer. So how's a couple to get there? How do you get there when I am suggesting that you not pray with your engaged loved one privately? Later on in this chapter I'll provide you with a method for you to begin to practice.

It is important that your personal prayer life be intact and as vibrant as much as possible. The Bible tells us, in Mark 14:38 to watch and pray so that we will not fall into temptation, and in Luke 21:13, to always be on the watch and pray that you may escape all that is about to happen. As you're preparing for your wedding, you are probably taking great care in arranging a band or DJ, making sure all the tuxes and/or the dresses are purchased or rented, or making sure that the venue is exactly what you want, with the right kind of food, etc. I encourage you to take as much care in making sure that your prayer life is where it should be before you marry. A lot of times couples come for pre-marriage mentoring with the idea that they may never have any other problems in their lives. Be assured, that within the first year there will certainly be something that is not fully agreed upon that will challenge the two of you. To not have some method to talk about things, and to pray about things, is a recipe for resentment to build in your young married life. So as you begin to pray for your wedding day, and for your marriage, what are the things you are praying about? Have you taken the time to look within yourself and ask God what is it He would have for you to be a good husband, or a good wife? Prayer needs to cover the entire part of your marriage relationship. God is in charge of our entire life, not just the life that we choose to show Him. So begin today to pray for all the aspects of your marriage life. Pray for the place that you and your spouse will live. Pray for the kind of church fellowship you should experience. Pray for how you will serve the Lord together. Pray for your finances. Pray for your intimate life. Pray for your prayer life. Pray for a relationship that is filled with honor and honesty, genuineness, and forgiveness.

You can be certain that if your prayer life is not active in your marriage relationship, your communication will be equally inactive. Just as you must have a plan for other areas of your married life, you need to have a plan for your prayer life. As I've written, I used to pray with my wife in the evening just before we would go to sleep. During my graduate studies, I was studying a book on Pre-Marriage Counseling, entitled,   <u>Pre- marriage Counseling</u>

With Temperament, by Dr. J. Terry Twerell. My wife and I were traveling on a plane while I was reading his book. My wife looked over my shoulder and asked, "When are we going to do that?" After a brief discussion about what the "that" was that she was talking about, I decided that we would begin that evening. I give credit to that author, and that one page, as it changed how I prayed with my wife forever.

The author suggests a couple seek agreement, and be purposeful, in how they pray with unity. I recommend to the couples I work with that they spend time writing out their prayer needs before they come together in prayer. By first thinking about their needs and writing them down, the couple will individually come to an understanding of their needs. When they come together for prayer they spend some time talking over what they have written. This process allows the couple to work through their prayer needs with God before they come together, and then seek agreement over their needs as a couple. Discussions about the prayer needs become prayerful by themselves and allows the Holy Spirit to work with the couple in finding God's will. For so many years, my wife and I prayed for each other and really thought we were praying effectively and in a God-honoring way. As it turned out, there were some areas that we were praying about that we were not in agreement. We were not necessarily in disagreement, but we weren't really in full agreement either. Dr. Twerell states, "the power of agreement is the foundation of Christian marriage." (Twerell, 1997) For many years in our marriage my wife worked outside the home, and still does. During this time in our marriage my wife commuted an hour and 20 minutes each way. We would regularly pray about her job. I later realized that I was praying for promotions and a raise, and she was praying for a new job. When we began to pray about my wife's job situation with unity, God blessed us by providing my wife with a job 5 minutes away from our home. Since we were able to begin praying with unity God was able to respond. It seems that to this day I still wonder why I had not been obedient long before. I realize it was because I did not have a plan for prayer. I am thankful that God doesn't withhold blessings from us just because we're slow learners. As you prepare for marriage, I really encourage you to begin to pray with purpose. I encourage you to pray with a plan and include all the aspects of your upcoming marriage life. My wife was blessed to reclaim three hours of her day for the family. I was blessed to have my wife for another three hours a day rested and alert.

In your preparations for marriage, I encourage you to be aggressive about having an active prayer life. After you're married, I encourage you to be aggressive about having an active prayer life as part of your marriage relationship. Couples might have to start off with the strategy by using it only one day a week. The unity accomplished on that one day can be carried over to the rest of the week. The prayerful discussions to reach unity will lessen the apprehension that some couples have in praying in front of each other. It has always been challenging to my thinking that married couples can see each other with their clothes off and be alright with it, but ask them, especially husbands, to pray with their spouse and they act like you asked them to run through the street naked. Marriage is so special in providing a connection to God, the author of marriage. Satan has done everything he could to turn the marriage vows and the marriage relationship upside down by making prayer some deceptively mysterious situation.

As you prepare for marriage life, and you work at increasing your individual prayer life, please know that couples that pray together daily have a greater chance of staying together. The following is the prayer strategy format that I use and give to couples. I hope it is helpful.

As an engaged couple you would follow all the steps except the time of physically praying with each other. Your discussions toward unity may happen outside the presence of your mentor couple. Be very aware about Satan's attack. If temptation arises, you should confine your discussions of unity, and your prayer time to those times when your mentor couple is present. I understand the push back on this concept. Many engaged couples are in love with each other, and have a passion to honor God. A simple question to ask yourself is this; When you take

time for prayer with each other how often does it turn in
to something more like a "make out" event?

Prayer Strategy

The core Christian marriage lies in the understanding of
Matthew 18:19 "Again, I tell you that if two of you on
earth agree about anything you ask for, it will be done for
you by my Father in heaven. For where two or three
come together in my name, there may I be with them."

The power of agreement is the foundation of
Christian marriage. Two people, who are close enough to
share intimacy and life have an ability to walk in
agreement. No other relationship is as powerful in
agreement as that of the husband and wife. Satan knows
the effectiveness of the power of agreement in Christian
marriages and works overtime to destroy the couple's
prayer life. For most Christian couples, finding the time
to pray together is thought to be hard. Alternatively, they
find prayer together in their marriage is an awkward

process. Who leads? What do we pray for? How do we pray? How long do we pray? These questions, if left unanswered, cause prayer to stop in the marriage. An effective approach to bring agreement into a marriage is as follows:

- The couple should agree on one or two mornings, or times, a week to pray together.

- Prior to this time each partner writes out specific things each desires to pray about during the prayer time.

- When they come together each partner reads their prayer list aloud, and explains his or her desire.

- Questions are asked, and understanding is established before formal prayer happens, thus the development of a prayerful attitude. This promotes that goal of the power of agreement, and is instrumental in achieving success.

- After both have read their list the couple holds hands and prays for the expressed needs. (I have noticed that some couples alternate praying for all the needs, and other couples pray for their partner's list. Either is acceptable as long as there is agreement with the couple.) For couples who are new to the concept of praying together I suggest the husband assume his God given role, and lead.

- After praying about the lists the couple may stay in prayer together, or separate for time of individual prayer.

A personal note to men: if you want to experience the pleasure of your marriage it must start with your prayer life. I found great joy in seeing my wife's comfort when she knows that she's been heard, and strengthened.

Another aspect of marital prayer life that it took me to long learn was what time I prayed with my wife. As I've written I would spend evenings before going to bed praying with my wife. I always thought I was obedient, and I always thought it was God-honoring. After some personal prayer I came to realize that I had, in fact, relegated those parts of our marriage life that are the most important, our prayer life, to when I was most fatigued. So we began to do our prayer time, and our study time, in the mornings before we left for work. Granted, it was a little bit difficult and initially a little different, but it actually turned out to be a real blessing. One morning, as I was praying with my wife, I looked up and she was crying. For most guys, I guess they would react like I did and ask, "What did I do wrong?" My wife looked at me with only the gentleness that she can look at me with, and stated, "It just feels so good to know that I am covered in prayer for the day."

There is no way that I will ever return to praying with my wife only when it is convenient. Why would I deprive myself of such a blessing each day? Our prayer

15

life is filled with intensity, love, and laughter. It is truly the greatest way to start the day.

You are getting married to spend the rest of your life with the person that God has brought into your life. You want to have a successful and vibrant marriage or you would not be reading this book. Please remember this point. For years we have known that an active prayer life between married couples is almost a guarantee for success. In the 1980's, probably before you were born, studies showed that couples that prayed together had a less than 1% divorce rate. The breakdown was one out of 1156 opposed to the 1 out of two that exists for most others.

In their book, <u>Couples Who Pray,</u> SQuire Rushnell and Louise DuArt provide some encouraging data regarding couples who pray sometimes versus those who pray a lot.

*For those who pray sometimes, their happiness with marriage is 60% versus 78% of those who pray a lot, viewing their marriage as happy.

*74% of those who pray sometimes say they are very happy in general versus 91% of those who pray a lot.

*Of those who pray a lot 77% say "My spouse makes me feel important." versus 59%, who pray sometimes.

One piece of data that jumped out at me was that there was a 30% difference in the agreement that "my spouse delights in me," 30% more feeling of delight for those that pray together a lot.

With that knowledge you have to ask yourself why you wouldn't pray with your spouse every single day. Preparation starts before marriage in your individual prayer life

Action Items

- **Identify and interview your prospective mentoring couple. Examine your prayer life to determine God's will.**

- Work with your mentoring couple to gain an understanding of the prayer strategy described the book.

- Develop unity in your wedding plans by using the prayer strategy to discuss any issues while meeting with your mentoring couple.

On Your Way To Delight!

With your first glance of the above title to this chapter you might have thought wow we start off the discussion with the most intimate part of the marriage relationship. Well stay focused, because this is the most intimate part of your marriage relationship. And that is the delight in yourself that you must develop in order to be a delightful partner, as well as to find delight in your spouse.

There is absolutely no place in my mind that would allow me to accept the idea that a person can have a healthy and fruitful love relationship with God, or another person, if they haven't developed the knowledge and ability to delight in themselves.

Some verses that I am very passionate about are Psalm 139:13-14. In my many years in ministry I have found, and continue to find, that many people in church are familiar with these verses when I start to recite them. The verses are often quoted in churches. What usually baffles me is that the verses to paraphrase them teach us that God knew us before we were knitted in our mother's womb that we are fearfully and wonderfully made, and all of God's works are wonderful. Very few people that I have encountered have a problem recognizing these verses, and many can recite the verse along with me. The part of the verse that eludes most people is the part of the fourteenth verse that makes the whole passage come alive for me. Some translations state it as "I know that full well" (New International Version); some state "I know it with all my heart" (Good News Translation); or "that my inner self knows right well" (Amplified Bible), or "...my soul is fully aware of this" (God's Word Translation). I interpret this last part of verse 14 to mean that it is the essence of who a person is. Because you know how fearfully and wonderfully made you are you should strive to live in a way that the world will see that you are comfortable, and even delighted with how you are made.

If you are planning to marry, or enter into any deep relationship, it is important that you examine your level of delight with yourself. Again, there is not a place in my mind that allows for someone who is planning to marry to develop a deep God-honoring relationship without being genuinely delighted in how God has created them. A person cannot delight in someone else, and view that person as having no flaw, if that same person is hyper-focused on their own failings.

The process begins with an examination of just how fearfully and wonderfully made you are. If the previous sentence makes you squirm a little don't stress about it. My sense is that it should always make a person feel some energy when that person embarks on some self-exploration. This is especially true when that self-exploration has, as its purpose, the celebration of the greatness of God through the creation seen in the mirror every morning.

In order to fully complete this process I encourage you to connect with a ministry, pastor, or counselor, who

is trained in the use of the Arno Profile System (APS)
(Arno and Arno, 2002). I have used this assessment for
20 years. The APS has proven to be very accurate and
dependable in our ministry. It examines how God
created you based on Psalm 139:13-14 to determine your
temperament, and thus help you understand how your
temperament interacts with the world, and how the world
interacts with you. (Arno) The assessment examines your
need to be with people based on your expressions, and
based on your internal need. Under the area of control
the APS examines your need to tell others what to do, or
your need to allow others to tell you what to do; who has
the power in your relationships; or your will over God's
will. All of the areas help you learn to delight in how you
are made and will equip you to then teach your
prospective mate how to delight in you.

One of the areas that is examined with the APS is
affection. The profile helps you learn and delight in how
you give and receive love, affection, and approval to deep
relationships. It is easy to understand how important this

knowledge is in teaching your future spouse how to delight in you.

It really is fun. I understand that this short explanation probably doesn't do the APS justice, but be assured that this will be a wonderful experience of learning. It is important that your mentor couple is familiar with the APS and how the five different temperaments interact with each other. If your mentor couple is not familiar with the APS it does not mean they are disqualified. You can find a pastor, or counselor, in your area by contacting the National Christian Counselors Association, or NCCA.org. The temperaments, just for information, are Melancholy, Choleric, Phlegmatic, Supine, and Sanguine. Each temperament is uniquely crafted by the Lord providing for a lot of variety in relationships. The fun part is that you get to a great place of understanding who you are in the Lord, and you get to really know and delight in the person you love, and are going to marry.

For you to develop the ability to delight in how God made you and in how God made your future mate, will you allow your marriage to begin with the ability to meet your mate's needs at a level that many couples without the delight might never reach? This book is written with my deep desire for you to be successful in marriage. I have a desire that you will not spend the first few years of marriage trying to figure each other out. You will have had taken the time to purposefully learn each other. Sadly many couples who do not prepare find themselves struggling those first few years to learn about the person they thought they knew, and now live with. These same couples find reaching unity in any area of the marriage to be difficult, because they are just trying to survive.

Developing a delight in each other is integral to the God-honoring marriage. As you delight in each other you can achieve the goal of having a marriage based on "No Fault Assurance" (Lea, 2011).

"The play on the phrase "no fault insurance" is intentional. No fault insurance is a premise that states anyone who has harm or damage from an accident would have their own insurance pay for those damages. The question of who is at fault for the accident is of little use. A person handles their own response to the accident through their insurance company regardless of fault. A similar premise allowing couples to take care of their own stuff before trying to place the blame, or responsibility for their struggles on their mate should exist in our marriages" (Lea, 2011).

This "no fault" behavior is based on the Song of Songs 4:7. In my book for couples I encourage the couple to read the Song of Songs to each other after your wedding day. They are love sonnets and can be very sensuous. For this reason I suggest you make yourself familiar with the verses, especially 4:1-7. I strongly recommend that you **do not** read these verses to your future mate until after the wedding. Satan is waiting to attack and he will twist your thoughts to lead you to cross some emotional and/or physical lines even with Scripture.

25

I do recommend though, that you and your future spouse are able to read Song of Songs 4:7 to each other. I have found this verse to be extremely special. It is important to be able to look at one's spouse and know that you "find no flaw" in that person because as the verse reads "...there is no flaw in you" (Song of Songs 4:7 NIV). You have probably already figured out that for your future spouse to be at a place where he or she looks at you in your best time, and maybe your worst time, and sees no flaw in you will be very satisfying. It is not a free pass to behave poorly in marriage. It is a value of unity in the marriage that produces peace and safety. It is one thing in marriage that will always make you aware of God's majesty and your need to rely on Him. God looks at you as a Christian and focuses on Jesus while he does not see the flaw. As you prepare for marriage it is important for you to know that "if we are fault focused we will be fault intensive." Meaning that the thing we will spend the most time on is the finding of fault, both our own, and our spouse. In reading Matthew 7:4-5, you learn that we are to spend more time taking care of our stuff than to spend

the time trying to clean up another's perceived problems.
For most of us looking for the speck in another's eye is so
much easier than getting the plank out of our own eye.
Clearly this is not a behavior that you should bring into a
new marriage.

Imagine if you will that you arrive home after
having one of those days that cause you to want to curl up
in a ball. That person who greets you, the person who
loves you, and you love, is the very person who might get
the junk of your day thrown at them. Typically, the
human response to such a situation is to fight back.
Again, imagine, the unity in your new marriage is to "find
no flaw" in each other. That unity is blessed by God, and
you have a completely different evening than what many
couples might have in the same circumstances.

It is my prayer that you will take this revolutionary
thought, pray over it, take it on as a value, and begin to
practice it in your relationship.

So many of the nuisance arguments that happen in
the early years don't happen when this value is in a

marriage relationship. In my years in ministry, whether pre-marriage or marriage, the "he doesn't she doesn't" arguments are of such little consequence, and so dishonoring to God, that it makes me grieve. It is the failure to learn, and to develop, a more godly view point early in the relationship that causes couples to resort to the behavior they learned from their parents or others - behavior that just does not work.

It is important to learn a different way of handling whatever conflicts come about in your relationship. You should not presume that it is the other person's problem. Choosing to find no flaw in the one you are to be married to will be nothing, but satisfying.

Later in the book, more effective forms of communication will be discussed. As you work through your self- examination please do the action items.

Action Items

- **Identify and interview your prospective mentoring couple.**

- **Arrange to have your Arno Profile System assessment completed and reviewed.**

- **Study and begin to use "No Fault Assurance" described in the book.**

- **Begin meeting with your mentoring couple.**

Some insight that my wife and I found very helpful is to know that learning to delight in ourselves, and learning to delight our spouse, is a lifelong process. As you begin your journey to explore who you are in the Lord, and who your potential spouse is in the Lord, I encourage you to understand that this is a process that starts now and goes on as long as you're married, which is to be eternity. At a time when preparations for weddings take on their own life and the busy nature of planning becomes the urgency of the day, for you and your loved one to slowdown to think long-term might be difficult. In our work with couples, my wife and I, had an occasion where one couple is two weeks married, another is 20 years, and yet another was married 54 years. Each of these couples experienced great joy from learning daily how to delight in themselves, and how to delight in their spouse. So to think that you might get this done in a week, two weeks, or three weeks, or even a year is a little naïve on your part. But to know that you will constantly be growing in delight of yourself, and in your spouse, is to know the true blessings the Lord has prepared for you.

Harmony From The Beginning!

In the process of pursuing each other you and your potential spouse took great care with the words you used, or in the behaviors you showed. As the relationship continues you find yourself letting your guard down, so to speak. Those things you used to say that made your loved one smile and glow a little bit are now those things that you choose not to say, because you think they're just understood. The things you chose not to say earlier are now the things that you say that you really shouldn't say. It's difficult however, I contend, to maintain behavior and language that constantly affirms your loved one when it is not the core of who you are. By that I mean if one is only masking their thoughts and feelings, eventually that mask fades. Each of us must know that we need to transform the way we think, and the way we speak in order to constantly affirm our loved one. It is not just a

compliment every now and then. It's not just an
expression of gratitude when something good goes our
way. It's not even the idea that you compliment the
person we live with daily.   It is a transformation of heart
that allows us to speak words, and behave in a way, that
our loved one knows that there would never be a time for
disharmony in our marriage.

I relate a story of my own marriage that helps
couples to gain an understanding of what I mean by
disharmony. I had a particularly stressful day. Stress for
me means the opportunity to serve a lot of people. I'm
blessed to serve in full-time ministry, but it does become
tiring. My wife and son picked me up from the church
office so that we could spend time together while we went
to dinner. Early in the day, I asked my wife to take her car
by a drive-through oil change. Usually this is something I
enjoy doing, but I had too many things on my plate, and
too many time constraints. (A side note: my wife works a
full-time job outside the home as well as I do).   I was
really not concerned with her time issues as much as I was
trying to get something off of my plate. So, my wife stops

by and picks me up for dinner. Our son is in the backseat, and I was driving. Things were going just fine until I asked the question about oil change. "Did you get your oil changed today?" My wife responds, "Oh no, I didn't have time." Now with the sensitivity of a block of wood, I say, "So do I need to show you where the place is?" Without thinking, I had taken what seemed to be a great opportunity for a great evening with my family and thrown it, figuratively, out the window. You might imagine that our evening had a little stress after my statement. Yet, that was not the case. We had a delightful dinner together with laughter and fellowship as a family. It is important for me to mention that even at this point in history I do not remember those words coming out of my mouth. In my critique, I let my tongue just wiggle. In the book of James, Chapter 1, Verse 26, we read, "If anyone considers himself religious and yet does not keep a tight rein on his tongue, he deceives himself and his religion is worthless." I know now with great certainty that I did not fulfill what the Scripture calls for in that situation. In my fatigue, intentionally seeking to provide harmony in my relationship with my wife seemed to take a back seat to just fulfilling my needs.

My temperament is one that short circuits relationship interactions when it feels it has had enough. Temperament is not an excuse to behave poorly. Knowing and delighting in your temperament causes you to rely more heavily on the Holy Spirit, especially when your temperament is strained. Our evening continued to be a very pleasant experience with laughter and discussion. Even after we returned home that evening I had no idea that I had said such a harsh thing to my spouse.

The next day, when my wife and I were better rested, my wife came to me and asked if we could have a conversation. For most guys, this seems like an invitation to do battle. Yet, if you delight in yourself, and delight in your spouse, there is really nothing that can happen in your relationship that poses a serious threat. In our many years of marriage, and having worked with a number of couples, we have developed an attitude within our marriage relationship that allows us to have our challenging discussions. The "hard talk hour," or HTH, will be discussed later in the book

As my wife explained the evening several things came to my mind. First, was that I still had no idea that I said such a harsh thing. Some of you may be saying if this is the harshest thing this guy might say then you cannot relate to me. But you have to understand the context of the statement. My wife and I choose to never have disharmony in our marriage relationship. So, for me to challenge her in this way was indeed harsh. It turns out to have become a very valuable lesson for us, and for other couples with whom we work. We learn to really be protective when we are tired, and never do the hard talks in the evening when were most fatigued. Second, the amazing thing that I noticed was when I asked my wife why she didn't say anything last night, either in the car, or at dinner. She responded with the grace with which she usually responds, "I knew that you would never do anything intentionally to hurt me, so I just waited."

In Ephesians 4:2 we read "Be completely humble and gentle; be patient, bearing with one another in love." I'm sure that when most people read this Scripture, they come to understand that to treat anybody, in any relationship, in a completely humble and gentle way, and to be patient, bearing with one another is the ideal way to behave. Isn't it all the more so in our marriage relationship, that we treat our spouse in such a way as to provide a safe atmosphere, filled with patience, gentleness, and love? Understand that at first glance, the Scripture seems like a tall order. However, we need to remember that this is a humbleness, gentleness, and love that is expressed to the person we love, who would not do anything to intentionally hurt us, and in whom we have found no flaw. We might even think that we have all rights to proclaim an offense occurred against us, or that the person has not met our needs the way they should. Yet isn't it more edifying to humble ourself so our mate can receive us when it is time to go to them than it is to just fulfill our immediate need to be right?

Another source of harmony in the marriage relationship are the words we choose to say to each other. I'm sure that anyone reading this book, or for that matter almost anyone, would say that being honest is a tremendous attribute for one to have. For most of us, honesty in a marriage relationship is what's expected. The experience I have with helping couples, and even in my own marriage relationship, is that the words we choose are not always accurate. In fact, some of those words are so inaccurate; they appear to be intentionally misleading. I tend to be a very black and white person, so when I write that these words appear intentionally misleading, I mean it. This often frustrates some people because they don't want to face the fact that they may not be an accurate communicator with their spouse. Ask yourself these questions: Are the couples you know filled with truth and honesty? Will your marriage be filled with truth and honest answers? Do you desire to be one of those couples who use the phrase, "I do not want to hurt my mate's feelings, so I do not tell the truth about what I'm feeling", as a way of doing life together? Do you envision marriage confrontation to be avoided at all cost, or as a prominent part of the couple relationship? Does the mere mention of the idea that you would have a hard discussion with your prospective spouse make you cringe? Are you the kind of person who screams first and ask questions after the pain has subsided? Are the marriages that you have been exposed to filled with the emotional darts used to keep the two of them in line? Emotional darts are those things we choose to say that are hurtful, and other things that we know will hurt because of the closeness we feel towards those with whom the darts are thrown.

It is probably safe to say that right now in your relationship you and your prospective spouse go to great lengths to choose the right words to affirm each other. Often, the tragedy is that as life comes, so does the lack of effort in protecting the words we use. Proverbs 24:26 states, "An honest answer is like a kiss on the lips." Honesty is an interesting concept. For many people, honesty is just the absence of telling a lie.

But I contend, in the marriage relationship, honesty means to accurately choose the words we say to our spouse in a way that clearly helps them understand what we are thinking and/or feeling. So many times I've sat with couples and heard words just thrown around, filling up the air, almost with an underlying intent to not communicate. There it is, that word, *communicate.* As you plan to marry, communication seems so easy. And it probably is very easy right now. You spend a lot of time taking care of the words you use, and listening to the person you are going to marry. Yet, as life comes good communication seems to wane. As things get more comfortable, couples begin to use shorter words, fewer words, more non-descriptive words, and even sometimes lie. We do not speak with precision, and yet we expect our loved ones to be accountable for knowing whatever it is we are feeling or thinking. Many couples might find themselves, later in their marriage, blaming the lack of communication as the reason for any problems that they experience. To a great extent they are correct.

I have often related a story about a friend who had
loaned me some golf clubs with the hope that my learning
golf would allow us some more time together. I kept his
clubs for about a year while I took lessons, and went to
the driving range. I never took the opportunity to go to a
golf course and play a round of golf. After a year or so I
took the golf clubs back to my friend and proclaimed, "I
am quitting golf." He looked at me with little emotion
and stated, "You can't quit something you have never
started." He was right. I had decided to stop playing golf
when I had never even started. I didn't want to spend the
time it took to play; my understanding was it takes hours,
to play a round of golf. I blame the amount of time
required for my not wanting to play. The big problem
was that I really didn't have an experience to be able to
say it took too long. So I could not logically say I was
quitting when I had never truly started.

My experience is that couples are correct when
they state that the lack of communication is the reason for
some of the issues that they experience. The problem is
that they are blaming something that they have never

done, that is, to communicate. They have not taken the time to work at experiencing communication; so it is not logical to blame it for the struggles in a marriage.

We use these words that seem to mean nothing with a lot of emotional meaning attached. One such word for me is the word *upset*. It's a word we hear a lot. You hear it on TV, and on the radio. You hear it in conversations to describe a large amount of feelings and thoughts. As you do your own self-examination, I ask you to do this one task. Take out a blank sheet of paper and draw a circle on it. Just above that circle write the word *upset*. Now take the time to write your definitions of *upset* in the circle. Brainstorm on the many things it might mean. Some examples are mad or frustrated. Now take that step one step further and ask some people close to you for their definition of the word *upset*. As you write all these definitions in that circle, I hope you become aware of the idea that you use the word *upset* for many feelings or thoughts. It is one of those non-descriptive words that just doesn't make sense. I have noticed when I work with couples that it is not just that it doesn't make sense in that particular moment, but that it makes no sense at all to the person, who receives the word *upset*. And in some cases it's a word used to hide what is really going on inside of the person who is sending the message. It's not that the person is openly and intentionally deceptive, but it is that they don't want to own what's really going on inside of them with the person that they say that they love, so they use the word *upset*. As I work with couples I watched one person, or the other, use the word *upset* in such an intensely emotional way that it's difficult for me to discern what it is they're trying to express. On the other side of that, I ask the person that received it, the spouse to whom it is said, to define what they heard, and what the word *upset* means to them. Most of the time the definitions are not the same, and sometimes they're even opposite definitions. As you've done your own self-examination about the words you use, and have found other people's definition of the word *upset*, it is important to sit with your prospective spouse and ask that person for the definitions of the word *upset*. In my home we have agreed not to use the word *upset*. It is such a vague word that I view it personally as a misrepresentation of any feeling I might have. I desire to know what my spouse means when she says something. I also desire that she know what I mean when I say something. It just does not happen with the word **upset**.

In the marriage relationship, the desire to be known by the person to whom you delight, and the person who delights in you, should be of the highest priority. Using honest words, clear and descriptive words, is essential for being known. The absence of such words tends to lead to nuisance arguments. "What do arguments prove and how painful are honest words" (Job 6:25). Take the time to examine other words you might use regularly in your relationships that do not adequately express the truth about your feelings or thoughts. Afterwards sit with your prospective spouse and share these words as well as share with each other the words each of you use that are non-descriptive, vague, or even dishonest.

Being honest with each other is God-honoring and couple gratifying. Maintaining harmony in your marriage relationship helps to ensure success in the marriage. One of the most important aspects of maintaining harmony in your marriage relationship is to provide a plan and a method by which you and your spouse can talk about the hard things that come up. There are two people in the marriage, and you can be assured that at one time or another you will disagree on small or even large issues. My wife and I have developed what we refer to as the "hard talk hour," or the HTH, or him to her, her to him hour." This hour should be on your calendar with a particular time during the week where you spend the time talking about the hard things of your relationship. These hard things aren't necessarily things that are emotionally troubling. They may be the things that need to happen in your relationship that require unity and agreement, like vacation time or a particular purchase. They may also be those emotional things that have come into the marriage relationship that require some fine tuning, some tweaking, or some abandoning. I recommend a set time for couples to spend time talking about those hard things. Maybe a Tuesday night at 7 PM, Wednesday night at 5PM, or it may be a Saturday morning at 8AM. It should never be any time on a Sunday. The Sabbath is supposed to be to build you up. To schedule the HTH on that day destroys the benefit to your marriage. The "hard talk hour" are essential for the health of the marriage. I find a couple stays in a state of unresolved stress without these planned discussions. The chance of success in a marriage is increased when the couple has an effective way of expressing their heartfelt views on subjects with the comfort of knowing that their mate has actually heard them, and responded appropriately.

As Christians we have a responsibility to resolve our differences in a God-honoring way. Couples, who have Christ at the center, need to implement the "hard talk hour," and not give up. Initially, it seems very hard and very cumbersome. For some people it also seems a little silly to sit and spend an hour talking about the hard things that may be going on in your relationship. It's important to remember that this is not about keeping

45

score. As we'll discuss later, there is a responsibility for each person in the couple to resolve their own issues with God before going to their mate. This is the most important part of the "hard talk hour." Practically every couple I have worked with have found that the setting aside time to discuss the things of consequence has produced tremendous results. The thing that especially pleases me is that if something happens on Thursday evening, that I've chosen to draw offense to, and I know that my "hard talk hour" is on Tuesday evening at 7PM, I have an obligation to go to God and get the plank out of my own eye before I try to get the speck out of my wife's eye. The time with the Lord is usually so gratifying, and so eye-opening to me about who I am and what's going on within me that when the time for the "hard talk hour" arrives the need to bring up several things on my list goes away pretty quickly. There are times when, in my hardness, I can't get through something; I have to bring it to my spouse. The joy of knowing that I'll be heard, and that she will be loved through that hearing, makes it so much easier. In reading Ken Sande's book <u>The</u>

Peacemaker, conflict should be seen as an opportunity to share Christ. I think conflict in the marriage relationship should be seen as an opportunity to deepen and strengthen the love relationship even greater. It doesn't have to be a "win at all cost" situation. It doesn't have to be an "ignore so I don't lose" situation where someone in a relationship knows that addressing a situation will not produce a good result, so the person ignores the offense without resolution. I am reminded of a statement my wife made during a mentoring session that went something like, "I don't want to argue with him because he can make the illogical sound logical and be my fault." Addressing conflict in that way does not produce the strengthening of the relationship that couples deserve. Conflict in marriage can be, may very well be, to gently restore my spouse and me with Christ at the center (Galatians 6:1).

Initially, the "hard talk hour" sounds like it is a little difficult, but once you start, it will become easier for you. Before each HTH each couple will write down what they want to discuss during the "hard talk hour." This is something they share only with themselves as they sift through things, and spend time praying. Seeking to be obedient to the Scriptures in Matthew that each person takes the time to examine their hearts regarding whatever might be the issue. An example would be if I drew an offense about a word that my wife used, and found it on my "hard talk hour" list. . The word could be harmless to most people, but yet creates a problem in my heart.

I have an obligation to my Lord and to my wife, to take the time to sift through why that word might be offensive, or why I chose to be offended by the word

I remember teaching a class of married couples and explaining to them that the words we use need to make sense to each other (Not all the words we use make sense to our spouse). We need to be aware of, and sensitive to the fact that words may communicate different things to different people. The reality is that everyone uses words (trigger or buzz words) that evoke a particular response. Trigger words is a fairly common phrase so I accept that the reader will understand what is meant by it.

The problem I have is that it gives a lot of power to a word.

Even now, as I think of a particular word, it makes very little sense for me to bring it up because for so long it would cause me to stray away from whatever relationship I might be having in the moment. For example, if my wife and I are having a discussion, whether intense or not, and the word "squirrel" was used, it would make me spiral for little bit. For most people, squirrel is a pretty harmless word. Yet for me the word squirrel takes me to the place where I've felt abused. The word was used to make fun of me as a child. My father used to call me squirrel as a means to beat me down, or inappropriately guide me. Whatever the reason, he used it in a way that didn't really feel good to me. I went through life believing that I had a real problem with my teeth regardless of how many people would tell me it wasn't true. The word, squirrel, still stirs within me some weird stuff with an emotional response. So you might imagine me having a conversation with my spouse about squirrels in the backyard and finding me a little off kilter. My wife had no

49

way of knowing the affect the word had on me unless I shared the truth with her. Now it doesn't bother me at all. But the point is that we all have those buzzwords that we tend to respond to without sharing them with the person that means the most to us; the person with whom we've chosen to spend the rest of our life. We find ourselves not sharing the impact of these words and then holding others accountable for having used the word.

Words have meaning and words are powerful. We have an obligation to our spouse to take the time to know which words make us respond in ways that may not be clear. I often ask my wife what I need to change or is there a particular word I am using that makes no sense. If it's a little bit hurtful, or even a lot hurtful, or just a word my spouse does not appreciate, my promise to her is that when she tells me a word that she prefers that I not use, I stop. Words are powerful, but they're not the only things I have to show my wife I care for her. It is action that says nothing is more important to me than what she values or what she desires. As you move toward marriage understand that if your spouse has a problem, it is your problem as well. Once things settle down both of you can talk about whether it should have been a problem or not.

What are the words in your life that cause emotional reactions in you? What are the words in your life that cause emotional reactions in your prospective spouse?

My recommendation for married couples is to identify an hour each week when both spouses agree to come together and share anything that might be bothering them. This is also a time, as I wrote before, that both spouses share what their desire is for vacation, or the purchase of a new car, or a particular difficult situation. For engaged couples my recommendation is for each person to take the time to go through the process and then do the first couple of "hard talk hours" with guidance from their mentor couple.

I understand that initially you, as a couple, might feel like you are being asked to show up for an argument session. Please be patient. As I wrote before, this is about you and your loved one taking the time to discern

what your issues are before you ever bring them to the
"hard talk hour." A great amount of time is spent
determining what you have to say, and why you're
responding to a particular issue. After that time of
reflection, a lot of things you think are important are not
and never come to the "hard talk hour". Many of the
issues resolve themselves and the "hard talk hour"
becomes time of love. After both parties have written
down their concerns and discussed them with the Lord,
they come together and pray. The things that are
discussed are things that may have been around for three
or four days, and you personally cannot overcome.

The hour is not done without a plan. There
needs to be a purpose to the meeting. This method has
shown to help remove those explosive events that happen
in the immediacy of the moment. Those "I feel, so I
express" moments that seem to show up a lot in
marriages. That "I feel, so I express" approach does not
usually produce understanding. What I've experienced is
that the "I feel, so I express" approach tends to produce
some other things that end up having to be discussed

during the ""hard talk hours". The "Hard talk hour"
happens at a mutually agreed time that is prayed over. It
is the time when both of you are rested and can relax in
an atmosphere of love. The "hard talk hour" should not
happen late in the evening when you are most fatigued.
I've never understood why couples would relegate the
most important things in their marriage relationship to the
night time when they are least able to accomplish
anything. Again, the "hard talk hour" should never
happen on the Sabbath. A personal preference of mine is
to not allow the encounters to happen in the marital
bedroom after you are married. The sanctity of that
room should be protected.

   Once the couple has determined the right time for
their hard talk they should position themselves on a sofa,
or similar piece of furniture, facing each other and
holding hands. With the couple seated, they remove the
power positioning that can often take place between a
man and woman. This positioning also takes away the
squaring off of the body, as if getting ready to fight, that
can usually happen in a hard discussion. Sitting also

removes that super unhealthy behavior of walking through, or out of a room, while saying something that is deeply emotional and hurtful to your loved one. This behavior never works, and most of us know it is plain selfish. It's when we throw that "word dart." A "word dart" is a word or two spoken in haste or under our breath that we know will hurt someone. When we say these words "**at**" someone the chance of arriving at one mind about the issue are slim. The bolding of the word "**at**" is intentional. The goal in a marriage relationship is to speak to, and communicate with, our loved one. You want to communicate effectively with the one in whom you find no flaw, and who would never do anything intentionally to hurt you. With the aforementioned being the goal, you should never have an "**at**" interaction.

Arriving at one mind, being united in the cause, being united as husband and wife, is the whole goal of the hard talk. Couples have to remember that it's vital to tell the truth in a way that each can embrace. While the couple is seated on the couch facing each other and holding hands, the husband should pray over the hour that they're going to spend together. The "hard talk hour" is an active way of loving each other. To pray and ask God's involvement in this hour keeps the three strands intact.

The process is vital. What I've noticed is that holding hands, looking into each other's eyes and facing each other provides several barometers for your loved one's feelings. When I look into my spouse's eyes during "hard talk hour" and see that she might be tearing up, or where she may be tensing up, or perspiring, I know that I need to slow down. It's also an indicator that I need to ask more questions and listen more intently. Often times, in discussions between couples, it's about data transfer. Let us get the information out as quickly as we can so that my need gets satisfied quicker and first. When you look into your loved one's eyes, and share honest thoughts and feelings, you soon figure out when you should slow down, or when you should just be quiet. Slowing down is an enormous asset when it comes to doing a "hard talk hour". Slowing down to a complete stop is sometimes necessary in coming into agreement, and in being united.

Experiences I've had personally and professionally have shown me that the faster people share, the louder they get, the more selfish they behave, the further away they get from coming to any resolution. Slowing the conversation down allows for understanding. Most couples will say that they embrace this "hard talk hour" concept. Yet when things become difficult they resort to their old-style. Admittedly, this style does not lend itself to immediate gratification. Within those two words, immediate gratification, there's an implied hidden word, <u>self</u>. The "hard talk hour" is a God-honoring method that tends to honor the marriage relationship more than it does the self. Taking the time to commit to the "hard talk hour" is work. It requires putting it on the calendar; it requires honoring the calendar; and it requires showing up with an attitude of love and openness.

An effective method used in the "hard talk hour" is something that's referred to as "reflective listening" or "mirroring". This style of listening can be hard at first, but after some practice the process becomes easier, and actually quite enjoyable. Many times I've found myself

56

sitting with couples and watching with amazement how long it takes one person when they try to repeat what was said. There have been so many times when a statement is made by one person and the words that come back are as if they were not even in the same room. I have been known to have a look of dismay at just how far off people are when they try to reflect.

We often use something as harmless as ice cream, or cottage cheese to have a couple discuss in order to get them in the right frame of mind about how to do reflective listening. On a funny note, even ice cream or cottage cheese can cause some tension in some couples. This is yet another reason to explore your own stuff before you try to share with your loved one. To explain, for example, I ask one person to describe their favorite ice cream. Let's say the person says it's chocolate chip. Typically, the one spouse will say to the other "I enjoy chocolate chip ice cream". The spouse may respond "You always enjoy chocolate ice cream". That's not what the spouse said initially, and so he or she has to repeat it until the person receiving the statement can actually

57

repeat it in a reflective way, exactly. They don't move on until the one who received the message can accurately reflect what was said. Some therapists, or pastors, will use passing an object back-and-forth before you have permission to speak. You do get to the place where you clearly can reflect what was said to you. The advantage of having the guidance of a mentoring couple during this time is that they can watch the way you interact, and they can show you when to slow down, while encouraging you to continue to repeat your statements until your spouse actually gets the message.

I've notice that women tend to give a lot more information than men can handle in the moment. I encourage women to speak in single sentences. Not because guys are not smart enough to get it, but because the guy processes on the basis of how he fix things. He goes into that mode after a few words. So the woman, by giving more than one sentences, is barely equipping her loved one to respond accurately by using so many sentences. When slowing down the process I've asked the woman to speak in single sentences until her guy is able to say exactly what she said to him. What has to happen is that each person (before they present their view of their thoughts and words) takes the time to sift through their own need. What is it that they really want to convey? Are the words they are using the words that make sense to them, as well as to the person with whom they're communicating? That's what makes the "hard talk hour" a little cumbersome. Initially, it is that we don't usually use words that make sense to other people. We use words that only makes sense to us, and we hide behind those words in a way that's unloving toward our loved one.

"I" statements are those statements where a person making the statement owns the thoughts and feelings being expressed without accusing someone else of being the cause of those feelings or thoughts. When someone is trying to send a message with the word "you" in it, the person receiving the message seems only able to defend. As much as people try to convince me that they are good communicators in the marriage, all I have to do is watch a little while when hard things are being expressed, to know that they are attacking with <u>you</u> statements.

A favorite verse in our marriage, and one we try to keep right out in front of us, is Ephesians 4:29. Ephesians 4:29 states, I paraphrase, that we should not let anything unwholesome come out of our mouths, but only that which builds up another according to their needs, to benefit those who may be listening. We're only to say those things that build up our loved one after we've taken the time to consider what our loved one's needs are, and to know that God, our children, and others are always listening to what we say. They will benefit by how we speak in a God-honoring and loving way to others. Certainly, attacking our spouse with <u>you</u> statements or accusations does not work. Following Ephesians 4: 29 in our marriage relationship, or for that matter all relationships, results in a tremendous reduction of stress.

In my marriage as communication skills increased, our "hard talk hours" became just time to love each other. We became so accustomed to the idea that we would have the discussions, and that we would be heard, that we began to work on our stuff, our personally chosen offenses, in a mature way, and they never came to the "hard talk hour." If things came up during the week, we moved through the issues alone in a healthy way. By the time the "hard talk hour" came around we no longer had the issue. Most couples come to realize that the reason for responding emotionally has more to do with their individual impression than it does with the intent of their spouse. Remember, the person, who is sending the message to us, the person we've chosen to be offended by, is the person to whom we find no flaw, and who delights in us while we delight in them. It is important to remember that we operate on the basis that one's spouse (or fiancé) **would never do anything intentionally to hurt the other**. As long as we operate on that basis the handling of conflict becomes more God-honoring.

In his book, The Peacemaker, by Ken Sande, I found the handling of conflict to be particularly helpful. I believe Sande presents tremendous information on conflict resolution from a biblical perspective. Every

couple we work with we recommend that they purchase
The Peacemaker to become well acquainted with how to
resolve conflict in a biblical way. One of the biggest
challenges in my life, and certainly one of the unhealthiest
behaviors in a marriage, is a use of this thing called,
sarcasm. I think people use this inappropriate
communication in order to mask feelings and thoughts.
In using this style, they confuse their spouse and create
chaos.

In the book of Proverbs chapter 26:18-19, we read
"like a madman shooting firebrands or deadly arrows is
the man who deceives his neighbor and says, I was only
joking." Sadly, many couples that we work with find
themselves in the "I was only joking" mode. As you
prepare for marriage, begin to examine whether you
operate in the, "I was only kidding", or "I was only joking"
mode. Do you find yourself saying things under the guise
of humor when you are really trying to effect a change in
your loved one? Do you find yourself saying things that
are potentially hurtful, and then dismissing them with "I
was only joking", or speaking in a way as to provide a little

truth and a little bit of deception, presented with a smile
while hoping that the person you say you love will figure
out what's really going on with you? We need to rid our
relationships of this unhealthy, and I believe ungodly,
behavior, as much as we need to rid ourselves of the word
"upset" and other non-descriptive, dishonest words. I
believe we need to rid ourselves of the use of sarcasm in
the marriage relationship. I don't believe sarcasm by
itself is harmful, but I do believe that sarcasm used in the
marriage relationship is very damaging. For many couples,
I think they have to see sarcasm as what I refer to as the
"language of Satan." Only Satan is honored by using a
little bit of fake humor, a small element of truth, put
together with some misguided need to communicate
some thoughts and feelings. Many couples find
themselves saying harsh things under the guise of humor,
and calling it sarcasm. What I know is that those words
go deep inside of us, and stay around a long time. We
may not react to them in the moment, but we will react to
them eventually. Some temperaments might respond

immediately whereas other temperaments might allow the sarcastic statements to go deep inside and fester.

We have real needs that we want to express to the people that we love, especially our spouse, or future spouse. When we use sarcasm that need doesn't get met. Most of the time the loved one who receives the sarcastic remark walks away with remarkably little new understanding of whatever issue has been conveyed. The push to tell the truth in marriage should be paramount (Ephesians 4:15). That same push to tell the truth in marriage will drastically reduce the number of nuisance arguments that arise. For those who use sarcasm as a form of communication nuisance arguments are really prevalent. Why do Christian couples allow themselves to entertain this kind of behavior? This is a communication style that is brought forward from their parents or from another married couple they know. As you examine who you want to be in your marriage, I offer, in the strongest and most emphatic words that I can write **to see sarcasm in the marriage relationship as the language of Satan, only**

meant to deceive, and maybe even view it in some cases as abuse.

When I was a child, I was raised in an environment where sarcasm was used daily in our family. That being true, I went into adulthood as a Christian, who used sarcasm to let people and God know what I needed. Consequently, what I needed was not really stated so that need went unmet. Learning to give up sarcasm and learning to tell the truth is difficult, but so important!

As you prepare for marriage, you undoubtedly know the value of using the right words with the person you love. There would be little chance of you having reached this place in the relationship if you and your loved one had never said anything affirming and loving. When you have an unhealthy form of communication, it will show up the more comfortable you become with a person. Granted, it should be the other way around, the more honestly and affirming you speak the more comfortable you become. It does not happen the correct way unless you have a plan. In addition to a plan to speak honestly, you have to value honest love talk in your heart. This requires training along with the surrender of some of the communication styles you brought into the relationship. Most of us would not buy a car, a house, or anything from someone, who spoke in this "gray," fake way. Yet, we do seem to tolerate such behavior in people with whom we are going to spend the rest of lives with. Just reading those last two statements should challenge you to say, "No thank you," to this kind of behavior. If it was that easy, I think everyone would have already done it. Until you are able to recognize this poor communication in yourself, you will not be able to be a more honest communicator with your future spouse.

Planning for a wedding provides great opportunities to discuss many things that require unity. The development of your "hard talk hour" with your mentoring couple is a wonderful training ground. Recently, I attended a special wedding of a couple that my wife and I had the privilege of mentoring. All weddings are special. This particular wedding was especially meaningful because everyone in attendance could tell that this couple had done a lot of work to prepare for their marriage. This wedding was a celebration of unity. Each one in attendance stated how wonderful it was to listen and see the evidence of love, coupled with a plan to be successful. Like all couples, they had to have some difficult discussions about life goals, individually, and as a couple. This wedding was a celebration of the unity already achieved by this couple.

Action Items

- **Take the time to create a value statement for harmony in marriage.**

- **Examine the words you use to ensure honesty. Rid yourself of using the word UPSET.**

- **Search yourself to identify your "buzz words" like the word squirrel referenced in the text.**

- **What level of sarcasm exists in your communication style?**

Can I Stop The Wiggle?

In every relationship, there are times when the people who are in the relationship have to decide whether to say something or not to say something. Sometimes "stopping the wiggle of the tongue" seems almost impossible. This is especially true in the marriage relationship. The Bible teaches us in the book of James that "A person who calls himself religious and yet does not keep a tight rein on his tongue his religion is worthless." (James 1:26)

Stopping your tongue from wiggling appears really hard. It is not as hard as you might think, but it is something (like other areas in the book) that takes both practice and a plan. With your focus on keeping a tight rein on your tongue (and not letting anything unwholesome come out of your mouth) you might imagine that there are a myriad of things that don't get said. Guess what? That is just fine because not everything we choose to say should be said, and if everything is said, it probably lacks in value.

What many have referred to as a revolutionary thought is the premise I promote: "Each spouse has to live with the idea that their spouse would never do anything intentionally to hurt them." I have found this to be really difficult for some couples, or at least one spouse, to embrace.

I shared the story of that one particular day I had maxed out my ability to be available for a relationship. I shared how after hearing my wife's description of the evening, I explained that I was wrong and asked for forgiveness. Things were resolved and now the phrase, "So do I need to show you where it is?" is one of our giggle points.

There will be times when words come out of your mouth that cause you to be just as dismayed as your loved one. Words that should never have been said, but once they are, you think, "How did that happen?" It can be frustrating to have to realize fairly, consistently, that you do not have control of your tongue. God understands His creation very well and has addressed this concern throughout the Scriptures. Take some time and read about Job challenging God, Moses questioning God's direction, or the disciples pushing back when Jesus told them what was to become of Him. When couples come together they select the words they use very strategically. As time passes, the ability or desire to protect the words they use is less of a struggle. The true joy of choosing more appropriate words replaces the old method of blurting things out.

My question for you who are deciding to marry is, "Where would you be in the same kind of situation that I have described?" Are you a "let it go and ignore" kind of person? Are you the "let us do battle now" kind of person? Are you the "pay you back with silence," and "hope you figure out what you did to me" kind of person?

Or maybe you are the, "I love you too much to keep anything between us" kind of person. Of course that is where you want to land. You have to prepare now **before** you are married. You might have enough opportunities after you are married to test it. I guarantee you that you cannot and will not develop this tool in the middle of something difficult. The method my wife and I advocate is the "hard talk hour."

Action Items

- Develop and practice the "hard talk hour" with your mentoring couple.

- Take some quiet time to evaluate your responses to your loved one over the past week, month, or even hours.

- Identify those times when you decided to be offended.

- Examine whether you moved too quickly to satisfy your need without considering the condition of the person with whom you are talking.

- Determine those offenses you are to give up and
  those past responses with which you should seek
  forgiveness.

When Things Get Rough

So far, we have discussed several ways to develop God-honoring relationship tools. The goal of this book for engaged couples is to help you be prepared <u>before</u> you cross the threshold of marriage. Strong biblical relationships don't just happen because two Christians are marrying. In fact, the battle is often bigger when two Christians marry since both, or one of them, thinks that faith is all that is needed.

As you have prepared for the wedding, I am sure you have experienced some challenging conversations. Isn't that part of the fun of it? The intensity of the planning really will test your resolve to love this person, who right at that moment might be a little less than pleasant.

Just as the tongue can say," I love you," it can turn right around and pierce someone to their core. Proverbs 18:21 reads, "The tongue has the power of life and death, and those who love it will eat its fruit." Your tongue is a powerful tool in your relationship with your fiancé. Throughout the previous pages you have been encouraged to use more accurate words and stay away from gray words. You have been challenged to find words that show your delight in the person you are about to marry.

As you have read, you have probably made a mental commitment to change the way you say some things. You might have worked really hard to get rid of the sarcasm. One afternoon, you find yourself in the middle of a discussion about some issue that might mean very little, but the harmful words are flying right out of your mouth. Many times it is fatigue that makes it difficult to keep that tight rein on the tongue. You begin to question what has happened to you. You had thought you committed to not arguing, and yet you are in the middle of an argument. The delight you wanted to express to your loved one has been replaced with the need to win the argument. At least that is how it appears.

In all relationships there are stressors that might drive someone to be in conflict. Conflict is a normal part of doing life together. The sign of maturity, especially Christian maturity, is shown in how you resolve conflict. A testimony of love is to surrender your will to God's will in the middle of what might seem to be a battle that needs winning.

Just because you find yourself in conflict with your loved one doesn't mean that all is lost. It does not mean that you were not genuine in your commitment to change. Actually each conflict should be seen as a clear indication of your commitment to do things differently than you had before, and differently than had been modeled for you.

More recently, I remember one evening when my wife and I were expecting a couple at our house for mentoring. The original discussion of the menu for that evening was about lasagna. In subsequent discussions the menu had changed to baked ziti. I arrived home that evening and asked my wife if the lasagna was ready. She responded, "We are having baked ziti." Wouldn't you know, out of my mouth comes, "Gross." I have absolutely no idea where it came from, and it was in no way indicative of what I thought. Shortly after that, I heard my wife in the kitchen mumbling, "Gross, you said gross, gross is what you said." Her temperament had taken that mis-spoken word and started to run down the road to the idea that I must not like any of her cooking. As I walked to the kitchen, I had to understand that words, whether said accidently or intentionally, can cause harm. Since our plan is to resolve conflict differently, I approached my wife with gentleness, asked for forgiveness, and we agreed that a well-chosen question in the moment would have been helpful. Sometimes we hear things that causes some hurt. Much of that hurt could be prevented if we could state "This is what I heard," and ask, "Did you mean to say that?" The particular episode lasted about six minutes. It is now one more giggle point in our marriage.

If you do find yourself in such a situation you need to have a plan ahead of time to get back on track. Imagine your relationship as a train. The train and track system are a very effective way for getting work done. The tracks are designed to handle the maximum load at just the right speed. As long as the tracks stay intact, and the train stays on the track, everything goes smoothly. If a track breaks, or an obstacle is on the tracks, that is when there is a derailment. You want your relationship to be the train that never has any unresolvable problems. You don't want any derailments. Yet, derailments happen, and great work, often emergency work, has to be done to clean up the damage and get the train back on track. The work is not some haphazard process, but a process of strategy and implementation.

When your relationship gets derailed, you understand that getting back on track is attainable. You need to have a process with a committed plan in place before hand, and not rely on reaction. The process has to be done with purpose and in a God-honoring way.

I do not accept that this process is just to say, "I am sorry," and expect the world to turn right side up again. I know the statement, "I'm sorry", could be genuine and prayerfully thought through, but we all know that sometimes this is said to escape responsibility, or prevent something else from being said. We know even more that the phrase "I am sorry, I was just kidding" can feel like a figurative slap in the face.

Learning how to move away from "I'm sorry" to forgiveness is the healthy way to handle any offense. The idea of forgiving someone, or for that matter forgiving someone immediately, can feel like we are being robbed of our need to pay back. The fleshly desire for pay back only causes further deterioration of the relationship. Forgiveness brings about repair in the relationship.

A word of caution is important here to understand that this is not about changing the words from sorry to forgiveness. It is about the change of the heart to release an offense without demanding payment. God's example to us is that we were forgiven long before we were even aware of our sin. God's forgiveness is an act of love. In marriage the act of forgiveness is an act of God's love. God forgives without making us do some kind of ritual. He forgives when we will accept that forgiveness through the moving of the Holy Spirit. When forgiveness exists in a marriage, there is no need for a spouse to dance around for hours, days, or weeks waiting for their spouse to forgive. An attitude of immediate forgiveness is to be part of the fiber of a marriage.

For me, and for many people, there exists a practice of score keeping of the wrongs we think we have suffered. I had never truly considered the damage that "score keeping" was having on me. Being raised in a family that was very proficient in keeping score I had little choice other than to think it was normal. As I've mentioned my awareness of this issue came about for me while reading The Peacemaker, written by Ken Sande. A particular phrase in his book transformed my way of thinking. Sande writes, "Unforgiveness is the poison we drink, hoping someone else will die" (Sande, 2004). His point, as I understand, is that the resentment and bitterness that I held onto under the practice of "score keeping" was eating me up inside at various levels. This "score keeping" behavior was damaging me emotionally, physically, relationally, and spiritually. In the Greek this persistent, low level anger, is referred to as "orge." It is a slow burn that tends to fester inside the person. It is an anger that separates a person from others. It is also an anger that separates a person from God.

There certainly are times that anger can be appropriate, and maybe even righteous anger. This is anger that does not express itself in a sinful way. I must say that there are not many people that I have known that can express anger in a godly way.

One of the difficulties with anger is that anger is often the most widely accepted emotion in the American society. We appear desensitized to the expression of anger, and uncertain about the emotions of sadness, hurt, or frustration, etc. In our society, there is this expectation that if one is hurt, they will act angrily. If someone is sad, they express it with anger. Or, if a person is frustrated, they express it with anger. It is as if there is an underlying understanding that many emotions are stepping stones to anger. I know that this is not true, yet I know that someone will immediately express anger at times when another emotion is taking place. I reject any notion that they are connected, but that each emotion is a separate expression. What separates these emotions is the ability to tell the truth on what one is really feeling, or thinking.

Below is a visual of what I refer to as the:

Mis-steps to Anger:

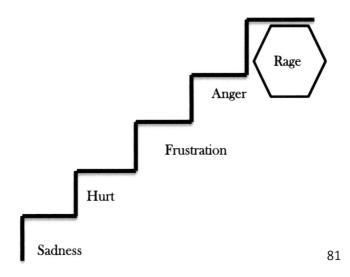

Rage

Anger

Frustration

Hurt

Sadness

81

Where are you?

Sadness | Hurt | Frustration | Anger | Rage

The mis-step is to think that there is a natural step from each emotion that leads to anger, and maybe to rage (that should never be used in a relationship). Hurts can and do happen in relationships. I suggest that each person take the time to genuinely determine, with accuracy, what they are feeling. I further suggest that you take the time to work on developing an attitude of forgiveness that allows for <u>immediate forgiveness.</u> Immediate forgiveness is the desire to behave Christ-like with the person you are going to marry. Immediate forgiveness is forgiveness without placing demands on the person forgiven to prove that they understand the level of your offense.

An examination of the story of Jesus and the two criminals on crosses next to Him will help you better understand the concept of immediate forgiveness. One of the convicted criminals says, "Jesus, remember me when you come into your kingdom." Jesus answered him, "I tell you the truth, today you will be with me in Paradise." (Luke 23:42-43) You notice that Jesus does not say, "Sure you will be forgiven, but first get down off the cross, and make things right." The criminal was not released from the consequences of his crime. The forgiveness given to him by Jesus was a result of genuine expression of faith from the heart of the criminal. When you examine your relationship to your future spouse ask yourself if you give him/her the grace that presumes a pure heart regardless of the actions expressed. You should learn to be eager and ready to forgive your loved one, regardless of whether they had the chance to work off their wrong. Understand that you have no right to compel them to, figuratively, get down off their cross and make things right before they are forgiven.

When working with couples, I use a tissue box to explain the process of forgiveness. The "Tissue Box of Forgiveness" (Copyright, 2010, Lea) helps create a clearer understanding of forgiveness, and is a good way to do self-check of your forgiveness toward others. I have provided a drawing of the tissue box with an explanation of the process. (Appendix A) With the tissue box facing toward you, and the opening facing you, start at the lower left corner. It is at this point that you identify the offense you have declared. A study of the word offense in the Scriptures shows that this could be something as small as a violation of personal space, or as large as murder. So you can see immediately, offenses are easy for people to create. What I find amazing are the behaviors and attitudes with which people choose to draw offense. An offense could be a tilt of the head, a laugh, a tone of voice, or just about anything else that someone chooses. As you prepare yourself, remember that you are protecting your future marriage from falling into the offense pit. This pit is that dark place that can develop in a relationship when both parties are heavily focused on being offended.

As you continue to look at the tissue box and move to the right you encounter the hole in the box to access the tissue. After you choose to be offended, your first response is a fleshly one. Your emotions may be ones of hurt, sadness, or anger. These emotions are your gut reactions, and if you spend too long in those emotions, you will develop a figurative hole in your soul. The great difference to understand is the opening that once served as access to fresh tissues, is now an opening where used and soiled tissues are deposited. These used tissues represent the unhealthy thoughts and feelings that you have developed over an offense.

Your goal is to push through these fleshly responses with prayer and counsel. After pushing through these sticky feelings, and moving across the bottom edge, you reach the lower right corner. The lower right corner represents you having released the feeling part of forgiveness and having entered into the decision part. The lower right corner represents your disappointment that someone would intentionally, or accidently, choose to do the chosen offense. When you think about this concept take some time to read the story of Adam's and Eve's betrayal of God's command. After these two went against God's command, one of their responses was to hide from Him when He came to have fellowship. God's response to their hiding was one that resembles human disappointment. If you will allow the latitude to think that God knew, so He would not be disappointed, but that God responds to us in ways that we understand. As God approaches the two in his disappointment, He asks Adam if he knows his state (Genesis 3:8). God does not immediately state the wrongs that have happened toward Him, though He already knew. He instead expresses His disappointment.

When we are offended, and can reach the place where we are genuinely disappointed in a person's behavior toward us, we have the opportunity to decide to forgive. Forgiveness is a decision. Forgiveness does not

rest on whether our fleshly emotions are still churned up.
Forgiveness is being disappointed, and figuratively, or
literally, falling to our knees, looking upward, and asking
God to help with the decision to forgive. The decision to
forgive will ignore the flesh, and honor God through a
decision to release the chosen offense. In the same way,
God chose to forgive each of us long before we were
born. Through God's love, He decided to forgive us
through the sacrifice of Jesus. If you think about God's
forgiveness, it really doesn't make sense. Maybe forgiving
those who had sinned before makes sense, but not those
who will come later and sin. In the same way, God's
forgiveness might not make sense to the human brain;
deciding to forgive an offense you have chosen might not
make sense. Nonetheless, the decision to forgive is
necessary, and is liberating. The decision to forgive is the
upper right corner of the tissue box. Imagine that in your
disappointment you go to your knees and look upward
toward God and decide to forgive.

   As you progress across the top of the tissue box,
from right to left, you are moving toward wholeness. You

show your decision to forgive by chosen acts of ministry, or acts of kindness, or praying that the offender's name would show in the Lamb's Book of Life (Revelation 21:27). The wonderful aspect of this part of the process is that after you have decided to forgive, and move toward wholeness, you will notice that the opening on the tissue box is sealed off. It is here that your obedience is rewarded, and you are shielded from the hole that contains those used tissues. Those fleshly responses that you had worked through will no longer have the power they had before.

So what happens when you are the one who has offended another? It is easy to talk about the offenses we choose to see. Seeing our own offending behavior doesn't come as easily. Interestingly enough, most of us appear to not have any trouble with the concept of immediate forgiveness when we might have harmed someone. Most of us might have to admit that we want that immediate forgiveness, without any self-examination. We want the "sorry and move on" approach.

For genuine remorse to be experienced there must be some self-examination. From many years of ministry I have learned the words "I'm sorry" really have little value. This phrase is sometimes used to tell another person to stop talking, or that you do not care to talk anymore. Saying you are sorry may be genuine, however, most of us know that it is a phrase that is as watered down as saying, "How are you doing?" to someone on the sidewalk you do not know. Most of us care very little about the person, as it is just something we say. How many times have you heard "I am sorry, but ...." The addition of the word, *but*, completely negates the value of the word "sorry." You wind up listening to the words after the word but more than you experience a sense of remorse and repentance from the person speaking to you. When we apologize for something, and attach a qualifying statement to the apology, the apology is diluted, or even negated. You have probably used this style at some point in your life. Your goal is to be able to go to your loved one and genuinely ask for forgiveness because you know and accept you were wrong.

The phrase that has proven to be effective is, "I was wrong, please forgive me." It is not about changing the words. It is about doing some self-examination and seeking guidance for where you got off track. Taking the time to examine the event allows emotions to settle, and provides time for prayer. Being able to convey that you were wrong takes away the poor communication style that uses, *yeah, but*, in an apology.

I tell couples that one of the expressions or names for God in the Bible is Yahweh. They should come to understand that an expression we use regularly should be seen as evidence of Satan. That expression is "*yeah, but*." Each of us should understand that using that expression is one way of inviting Satan to inject himself into the moment. It doesn't matter if the words are there, what matters is the form of expression that is used. For example: "I am sorry (*yeah*), *but* ..."; (*Yeah*) God loves our marriage, *but* ...": "I find no flaw in my spouse (*yeah*), *but* ..."; God did a good job in me (*yeah*), *but* ...." Well I hope you get the point. As you prepare for marriage please take the time to remove this faulty

90

behavior from your communication. It is time to learn to use a period in our conversation, and resist filling the air with words. Using a period is the tight rein on the tongue expressed in James 1:26.

As you have worked to identify your chosen offense, you have pushed through the fleshly responses, and reached disappointment. You sought God, and decided to forgive. You now find yourself moving across the top edge of the tissue box. You are shielded from the emotions that you had originally attached to this offense. You will begin to experience a new set of emotions, like peace, contentment, or relief. Through these chosen acts of ministry, you are working toward the upper left corner. This corner represents unity with God and **wholeness** in your spirit. No longer does the **hole** that was created by those used offenses have any impact. You come into unity with God and experience the maturity attained by experiencing the **whole measure** of the fullness of Christ (Ephesians 4:13).

Action Items

- Examine the words you use to express emotions, and determine their accuracy.

- Examine the ways of forgiveness that have been modeled for you.

- Become familiar with the "Tissue Box Of Forgiveness" to see your growth in forgiving.

- Confess and seek forgiveness for any offense that you have held onto.

- Let go of any *"yeah, but"* expressions.

- Decide to FORGIVE. Decide to accept FORGIVENESS.

Can Small Things Matter?

In this chapter you will explore three areas of the marriage relationship that may seem inconsequential. These three areas are very important for a healthy and God-honoring marriage. They are the value of laughter, Ecclesiastes 3:4; the importance of protecting connectedness, Isaiah 14:24; and managing what you model, 2 Thessalonians 3:9. You will note once again, that you need to have a plan to have these values in your marriage they do not just happen. .

In Ecclesiastes 3:4, we read there is a time to weep and a time to laugh. The area of focus for you is that there is a time to laugh. Laughter in a marriage relationship is priceless. Laughing with your spouse regularly is good for the body and the soul. Be cautioned though; this is not laughter at your loved one's expense. It is not sarcastic or cynical remarks with a giggle. The laughter that I promote is one that can be shared between a husband and wife in their most intimate moments, as well as those moments that produce a great deal of stress. While you are dating, you probably have a lot of time where you and your fiancé are able to laugh with each other. Since that is the case, you already know just how wonderful it feels to be in a loving relationship that has laughter as part of it. The importance of this attribute, you already know. It is the development of a plan to keep laughter as a primary component of your marriage that will take some focused intent.

A study done at the University of Maryland concluded that a person should have thirty minutes of exercise three times a week and fifteen minutes of laughter on a daily basis (Miller, 2000). This study also suggests that laughter could conceivably promote a healthy endothelium that reduces the risk of cardiovascular disease.

Laughter, coupled with balanced prayer, rest, and communication, will be good for the health of your marriage. Laughter helps provide the necessary release of the day's stuff in the same way as some other forms of expression. Those other forms of expression, i.e. yelling, moping, etc., tend to create damage that laughter does not create. As you consider this value now in preparation for marriage, explore whether there have been times when your responses to stressful situations were just silly. If you had taken the time to laugh at yourself, or the situation, you would have used less emotional energy and caused less hurt.

Married couples are no different from everyone else in that life sometimes comes running pretty hard at us. The concern is that married couples, who are bombarded with the stuff of the day, run the risk of releasing the anxiety created throughout the day by unleashing it at their spouse. You will need to be able to talk about the hard stuff of the day, and we have discussed some plans to make that happen. You can't ignore the things of the day after you are married any more than you can ignore them now. What I am suggesting is that you start to realize that the things that happen around us are typically out of our control, and might not REALLY matter.

I have spent years trying to help couples separate the events of the day by using the "90/10 principle." This idea has been around a long time and most recently championed by author, Stephen Covey. The numbers do not matter as much as the disparity between them; it could be 80/20, or 70/30. What seems to happen to us is that the smaller segment, that 10% of the information, is given so much power over us that it engulfs the larger segment, the 90% of the information, and in the end determines how we react. We should see the 10% category as those things that are pretty much out of our control like the sun coming up, the rain coming down, and other people's behavior. This category is the "so what" category and should be seen as just part of what happens. By reclaiming the 90% of what we take in (and how we process it), we can leave a great deal of our anxiety at the door before we greet our spouse for the evening (Lea, 2011). We can choose to Not allow the 10% to control our thinking and our actions.

You are planning to marry the person that God has placed in your life. You have to learn to resist allowing someone else, or something else, from coming into your marriage and stealing even a minute. Laughing at the "so what" stuff will increase the peace in your marriage. It will also increase the chances of your marriage thriving instead of just surviving.

To know that marriage also provides a glimpse into what it is like to commune with God should challenge you to examine whether your relationship with God has any laughter in it. As I write these words, I get a smile while thinking of the times when I have laughed with God. The smiles also come when I tap into a memory of hearing my wife laugh with me. Some temperaments have to work harder to see the humor in life. For me, I could be focused on the times when I didn't hit the mark, but those things are now in my "so what" category. It was a great lesson when I learned that the benefit of a giggle in the morning lasts the entire day, and beyond.

As you prepare to marry laughter needs to be part of your relationship with your future spouse. It may be hard to believe, but I think that laughter sometimes has to have a plan. In my marriage relationship I try to purposefully create laughter moments, or as we call them giggle points. It is great to keep my wife guessing and laughing. The giggle points are the things that my wife and I can call on from memory to get us through the day, or through a tense moment. One of the best things for me is that the giggle points are just ours. Most people would not see me as a person who has this value. I really do not care as long as my wife knows me as that person. I encourage you to share these special moments in laughter only with each other only after you are married.

One of the first things I gave my wife was a stuffed bunny. As I indicated, many times making laughter happen has to have a plan. Well this little stuffed bunny has been on a tremendous journey since coming into our home. One day, my wife came home from work to find this bunny looking at her through the window of the washing machine. It was as if it was crying out for help.

On another occasion, bunny was caught in my wife's shower, and yet on another I rode around for a week before I realized that bunny had been strapped into our grandson's car seat for that long. I arrived home one day to find bunny situated with my guitar, as if it was playing it. Well, when my wife came home bunny was sitting in the corner with all of its paws bandaged from the punishment resulting from messing with my stuff. One last example is when my wife arrived home, and proceeded to go and change her clothes. When she entered the bathroom, bunny was sitting on the toilet reading the blue prints of our house. You can see that some giggle points take some work and planning. It doesn't have to be that elaborate. The episode described with the bunny sitting in the bathroom took some thought and some time. If I am asked, "Was it worth it?" The answer will always be "Yes!"

So many times someone in a marriage will bring home the 10% of the day and let it rule the evening. As you prepare for marriage, reclaim your 90% now. Decide today to be committed to having laughter as part of your married life. If a giggle lasts a day imagine how long a regular dose of laughter would last in a marriage.

I am always in awe of the way God creates balance in life. Laughter is such a healthy attribute to have in the marriage relationship. Laughter really does balance things out in a relationship. Laughter is beneficial for your physical body. Studies have shown that laughter actually strengthens our blood vessels and makes us healthier. Again, in a study from the University of Maryland, researchers concluded that 30 minutes of exercise three times a week and 15 minutes of laughter a day would create a healthier body. So as I see it, what God has deemed to be good for our physical being, He has also deemed it good for our relational being in the marriage.

As you think about your upcoming marriage, you probably have a hard time thinking that you could ever find yourself disconnected from your loved one. What I have noticed is that couples drift apart from each other when they are not purposeful about staying connected. The phrase I usually use with couples is that this dilemma happens 'one shoe at a time'. One or the other begins to develop some separateness in their married life that results in greater and more serious distance. When a couple is dating, or first married, there is an energy between them that drives them together; they want to be connected. Regrettably, if there is no plan to stay connected, to keep the flavor of the relationship vibrant, the couple loses both the flavor, and the connection.

A new marriage begins with its own flavor that was developed while the two people were dating. That flavor becomes the thing that each of them looks forward to tasting. It is much like salt, when it becomes part of a meal. The meal has its own flavor, but the salt creates something different, and in the case of a relationship the added flavor raises the level of energy. Salt lets a person know that it is in a meal. In fact, salt can take over the flavor of the entire meal. Now what happens? Over time, the salt loses its ability to effect a change in the meal. Does it really lose its saltiness? Not really. What happens is the person using it becomes so comfortable that they don't pay attention to it any longer. Some alternatives are to put more salt into the meal, or maybe, take the time to be purposeful with the meal to create more flavor and enjoyment.

The marriage relationship might suffer from the same kind of stress, and start to lose its flavor. You are dating now without investing a lot of focused energy into each other because it is almost second nature. That energy will persist for a while after you are married, and you want it to last forever. The busy part of life will start coming at you. Maybe job stress, maybe children, or maybe anything. You might find that there is little time to maintain the flavor of your relationship. This condition doesn't happen suddenly. You have been intentional during your dating and early marriage, but have lost your intentionality to keep things vibrant. You have not lost your commitment to your loved one. The risk, however, is that you could lose your loved one by accepting a diluted or compromised marriage relationship.

In preparing for marriage, please remember that your biggest obstacle to a successful marriage is not always going to come at you with a big sign that reads "be careful." Satan attacks in a sneaky way to destroy what he hates, the institution of marriage. God created marriage; God loves marriage. Satan hates God, so therefore Satan hates marriage. It really is not hard to understand why he attacks marriages, especially Christian marriages so aggressively.

So many couples have described these attacks as hardly even noticeable. One of them "just" starts leaving some clothes in another room for convenience. Maybe one of them decided to open a separate bank account to have their own money to do their own stuff. One or both decide to have a guy's or gal's night out (without *being intentional about having a couple's date night)*. By themselves, these things seem harmless. But remember, you are becoming one with another person. How does separateness fit into oneness?

This discussion is not about restricting individuality. It is delightful that my wife enjoys different activities. I enjoy the fact that she has nights out, or

Michael K Lea
First Steps

weekends away with girlfriends. This discussion is about imbalance. If any imbalance exists, it should always be leaning toward the couple. The first time separateness happens it feels bad, almost as if one is being dishonest. Over time, the person becomes desensitized to this feeling, and ignores the stress it causes. In your present relationship state you have to be thinking this is silly, it will never happen to our marriage. That is exactly why you need to be thinking about it now. You can then have a plan to maintain passion in your marriage. For example, a man or woman decides that they would sleep better if they were in another room. This may be true, but I know from working with hundreds of couples that there is danger on the way. The marriage bedroom is a special place, so diluting it is dangerous. There may be health reasons or other concerns that can legitimize reasons for sleeping in a separate room. The couple might even agree that this is something they should do to "just" make things easier. The danger is the lack of planning to maintain the vibrancy that results from sharing a bed as husband and wife. A suggestion is that a couple

ALWAYS starts their night in the same room. Moving to another room for better sleep reasons can happen only after the plan to be close is in place.

Another example, and one that on the surface seems like it could not be harmful, is when husband or wife decides it is more practical to have their clothing in another room so they don't disturb their mate. How can this kind of thing be anything but considerate? Well, what I have learned is that Satan takes what started out as a practical solution and develops it into a destructive force. For most of us, when dating we did everything we could to be with our loved one. With this situation, things start out with some clothing in another room - figuratively speaking 'one shoe at a time' - and gradually develops into the idea that it would make sense to sleep in a separate room so the mate is not disturbed. The idea is that they are "just" trying to make things easier.

Over time, a husband and wife finds themselves tricked into thinking that there isn't anything left in the marriage; they "just" live in the same house. How sad this can be for the couple. As you consider your marriage, push yourself to not accept the things that look like they will "just" make things easier. Push yourself to accept only that which is JUST and RIGHTEOUS. Decide things on the basis of what is JUST for the protection of your marriage. The JUST thing is to make sure your marriage relationship is filled with, and covered with, prayer. The JUST thing is to consider your spouse's interest equal to your own (Philippians 2:4). Please work to not allow yourself to accept the small nature of the "just make it easier" approach. Be intentional and purposeful about protecting the flavor of your marriage relationship. There is a wonderful victory when couples take the time to have the right activities in place for maintaining and restoring the flavor of the marriage. The right thing, or the JUST thing to do, is not let the flavor leak out by "just" doing the easy thing.

If you have spent any time at all reading the Bible, you clearly understand that God is not a God of chaos. God is about having a plan. You know that not having a plan for a vibrant marriage is the same as planning not to have a vibrant marriage. Gradual deterioration can happen if there is no plan. The deterioration leads to a decline in honor and respect, and sadly the potential demise of the marriage. Isaiah 14:24 reads, "Surely, as I have planned, so it will be, as I have purposed, so it will stand." Allowing your marriage to happen purposefully provides stability and protection. God is glorified in the success of marriage. The planning you do now will provide for a legacy that impacts even your grandchildren.

A third area that engaged couples need to be aware of is that their marriage does not belong only to them. God uses marriage to bring other couples to a better place. The planning you do now for a healthy marriage will be used by God to draw other newly married couples to follow your model. The other side of the thought is that Satan desires to use marriages that struggle to influence others with questions of "why would they follow the model of a marriage that looks to be a mess?"

Throughout the Scripture, we read of Bible figures who took a stand to be obedient to God's direction that resulted in others following their lead. One way for you to take that lead is to continue to be your future spouse's cheerleader. Couples, who are committed to cheering each other along in a genuine way, are seen by other couples with a healthy envy.

To make the point, I can describe several occasions throughout my marriage where I had modeled a behavior that was not intended. My wife and I have taught together in mentoring, marriage seminars, and in prayer events and training. On more than one occasion my wife has been approached by other women, who expressed that they wish they had what she has. For the most part, the idea escapes my wife until the women explain that while my wife was teaching, these women listened to her. But they also noticed how much I was enjoying her presentation. These events model and teach a value that might well have been ignored if that value was not at the core of our relationship. That value is one of being our loved one's best cheerleader. Like so many teaching opportunities, the behavior we display shows more of our true selves than the words we might use. You should be aware that every place you and your spouse go in the future, there are nonbelievers and believers that are watching your marriage. As you have proclaimed a Christian marriage relationship you have also invited the criticism that Satan sets up when others see you stumble.

Within our society, there is a hunger for couples that can be emulated for healthy behavior. The difficulty is that many couples, even in our churches, tend to have a jaded view of marriage. Many people pay too much attention to the statistics on how difficult marriage is and lose sight of the victory that God has already assured them through His grace and love. To emphasize an earlier point, Satan hates God. God loves marriage, so consequently we have to remember that Satan hates marriage. The negative influence that Satan exerts almost makes it appear that people want marriages to fail.

In your preparation for marriage, I hope you can begin to see the wonderful responsibility God is placing on you. You are entrusted with a God created relationship that calls for your marriage to model strong Christian behavior. You are the shepherds of the Christian marriage model. As shepherds, you are entrusted with the sheep that God has given you. Those sheep, in this regard, are those couples who are watching you to see what is different. Just like the shepherd with his sheep great care should be taken to ensure they stay on the right path.

It should go without saying that this seems like a pretty big responsibility. Well, it is a great responsibility. It is also a responsibility that once it is understood, and you and your spouse are unified in your desire to serve God with your marriage, is easily attained. It doesn't take too much work to love each other in a godly way.

Christian couples are the shepherds of what they model to the Christian community and to the rest of the world. Couples know that they are the shepherds of their children, and that their children deserve to have parents, who are modeling success. Your actions must model what your words you say you believe.

In the book of Zechariah 11:17 there is a Scripture that reads, "Woe to the worthless shepherd who deserts the flock." The punishment described after that admonishment is pretty extreme, and I would encourage you to read it. As you read it, think of how devastating the response to the worthless shepherd is while also understanding that a Christian couple who doesn't model strong godly behavior in their marriage can be devastating for generations.

I believe the Christian marriage to be the baseline for a successful society. The strong Christian marriage that you are working toward will be very captivating to others. It will bring about some attacks to make you stumble. If you have worked through the suggestions contained in this workbook, and you have sought the counsel of a strong Christian mentoring couple, and most importantly, you have submitted your upcoming marriage to the will and guidance of God, you will be a tremendous model for others.

Action Items

- During this time of preparation for marriage, plan to develop healthy opportunities for laughter in your relationship.
- Preparing for a wedding and a life together is stressful. As a couple, learn to find some giggle points amidst the madness.
- Take the time to talk through your expectations of time spent with each other after married. Decide how much private time is comfortable.
- Develop an attitude of protection against anything that, or anyone who, might become a wedge in your relationship.
- Begin to talk about your marriage legacy.

God's Special Creation!

When working with couples, whether married or engaged, I try to impress upon them that the behavior that is exhibited in the kitchen is the same behavior that will be exhibited in the living room, and is the same behavior that will be found in the marital bedroom. So, if one person is selfish and self-centered in the rest of the house, it is certain that that person will be self-centered in the bedroom.

In preparation for marriage, I strongly encourage you to create purity in your relationship. If you find that you have crossed some lines of purity physically, it is important to step back from that behavior. Your desire is that God be there to bless all the parts of your marriage. If you are already playing at being married, you are restricting God's blessing. I am very challenged with the

history of failure experienced in marriages with couples
who are intimate before marriage, or live together.

The marital sexual relationship is an important
part of the marriage, but not the most important part.
The most important part is to glorify God with every part
of your marriage. God can't be glorified when His
directives are not adhered to. The blessing that God
places on this part of the relationship is as special as His
blessings in the other areas of marriage.

Sex in the marriage is for communication,
recreation, the edification of partners, creating babies, and
glorifying God. In the past, couples have tried to
convince me that sex before marriage is not a problem.
They want me to believe that it helps determine
compatibility. I don't agree with the premise that it is
harmless. I know God created marriage. He created it
for His glory. People may pretend that they have the full
blessings of God if they have sex before marriage, but they
don't. God will not go against Himself and therefore He
will not bless what He refers to as fornication. Sex in

marriage is beyond the mere fleshly desire created by hormones. It is God created, God involved, and God honored.

Returning purity into your relationship before marriage allows God to fully place His blessing on your sexual relationship with your spouse after the wedding. Imagine the blessing you receive when you pray together for God's blessing on your intimate moments. He created it, so certainly He knows how to make it great. It is a little humorous to think that we pray over our food before we partake of it, and yet don't pray over our intimate encounters with our spouse.

The marital sexual relationship provides for a oneness and connectedness between two people that is not replicated anywhere else in the human existence. This area of our marriage allows for a unity between a husband and wife not unlike the oneness that we are to desire with God. It is an area to be protected and respected.

As you pray about this area, remember that your role in this part of the marriage is no different from the other areas of the marriage. You are to seek unity through communication and prayer. 1 Corinthians 7:3 teaches us that "The husband should fulfill his marital duty to his wife, and likewise the wife to her husband." In fulfilling that duty, each party is to be focused on the need of their partner. It is important to be praying about this part of your relationship. Your mentor couple should be prepared to meet separately with man to man, woman to woman, to discuss how to honor God in this area. Do not place yourself at risk by having conversations about sex before the wedding night. You place yourself in a situation that allows Satan to slither in and say "You're almost there anyway, why not?" Corinthians also teaches that your body in the marriage is not your own. In light of this fact, you have an obligation to explore each other and ask questions about what pleases your spouse while at the same time teaching what your needs are. Again, this conversation happens after the wedding ceremony. Your satisfaction in this area is a direct result of your desire to honor God in all the other areas of your marriage.

Protecting this part of your marriage is extremely crucial. You should begin to safeguard your marital relationship now. Remove any and all threats to this area of marriage. Resist outside attacks from other men or women, and especially from the destructive forces of pornography. Pornography destroys the fabric of a relationship. Pornography disrupts and ruins a person's ability to see truth. Most importantly pornography is an affair. The use of pornography results in the breaking of the one flesh relationship that God has ordained for marriage. Many people try to reason the use of it away by stating it doesn't hurt anyone. It hurts one's relationship with God, and it hurts a marriage.

Action Items

- **Purchase a Christian book on the intimate nature of the marriage relationship. I suggest you** consider <u>Intended for Pleasure</u> by Ed and Gaye Wheat, Baker Publishing Group.

- If pornography is a struggle for either of you, seek counseling to rid your life of the danger. Deal with this before you enter into the marriage relationship, even if you have to postpone the wedding.

Final Thoughts

So you have been through this workbook and probably are closer to the date of your wedding. You have developed an awareness of yourself so as to move toward being the spouse God has called you to be. Your individual prayer life has been enhanced in preparation for the powerful nature of married couple's prayer life.

Hopefully you have examined your communication style to determine whether you accurately convey your needs, expectations, and desires. You understand that your particular temperament responds to the rest of the world differently than your loved one's temperament responds to rest of the world. The delight you have developed for yourself now enables you to truly delight in the one you are going to marry.

My hope is that these pages have helped create a path for a deeper relationship in Christ. All the tips and methods that are presented in these pages, or any other pre-marriage Christian workbook, are of little value without the truth that Christ at the center of your marriage is the key to success.

I know the hardest part about making life changes is getting started. Your desire and action toward preparing for a God-honoring marriage is what allows God to act. He often doesn't act until we take the first step on the path of obedience.

Take the time to consider whether the things you have been asked to do in this book are what God has called you to do. Seek counsel from your mentoring couple for other ways to honor God in your preparation. The Bible has shown so many examples of God's plan becoming real once God's people choose obedience. Please seek obedience over complacency. Please do not wait for the other person to act before preparing for success. You should consider the time spent in this book as the training toward a married life well-lived. The suggestions are time tested with many couples. You might not need all of them right now, but it is important to have a plan in place when you find yourself faced with the challenges that will come your way.

God created marriage for His glory. With that knowledge, you have the assurance that God will be the greatest cheerleader, if you will allow that term, for your marriage. He has gone ahead of you to prepare for victory and success. In the book of Judges there is the account of Deborah and an army commander, named Barak. In this account, Deborah assures Barak that God has called on him to take his 10,000 men and fight an even larger army. Just like your upcoming marriage, God is guaranteeing success, if you, like Barak, will show up on His side. Barak resisted initially, but eventually was obedient, and God destroyed the enemy. God desires that you show up, obedient to the call to invest in and protect your marriage. If you do just that, He will destroy the enemies of marriage. You will know, without a doubt, that God, just as Deborah told Barak, has gone ahead of you (Judges 4:14).

There has often been resistance to some of the suggestions you have just read. The one suggestion that my wife and I get the most push back on is the idea that engaged couples should not pray together. Remember they can pray for each other, but not with each other unless they are with their pastor or mentor couple.

Recently my wife and I were closing out a pre-marriage mentoring process. We asked the couple for their impressions and some things they had learned. In a very special way the groom to be said, "most guys talk about how they can't wait to wake up next to their woman. I can't wait to be able to pray with her." His bride to be seemed to melt with love because she knows how special that prayer time is going to be for them.

I encourage you to take your preparation for marriage as serious as you might be taking the preparation for the wedding.

May your marriage be blessed and may it be a testimony to the world of the God that has prepared the way for you.

References

Arno, R. & Arno. P. (2002) Creation Therapy, Sarasota, FL: NCCA

Covey, S. Retrieved from http//www.slideshare.net/Stephen-covey-the-90/10-principle.

Crabb, L.J., Hudson, D. & Andrews, A. (1995) The Silence [of] Adam: Becoming Men of Courage in a World of Chaos. Grand Rapids, MI: Zondervan Publishing House

Lea, M. (2011) So You Think You Are Married ...ten tips on how to live like it. Bloomington, IN: Westbow Press

Merrian-Webster Online. Web 26 Oct. 2010 <http://ww.merriam-webster.com

Miller, M. (2000). Laughter is the "best medicine" for your heart. Unpublished manuscript, Medical Center, University of Maryland, Baltimore, MD. Retrieved from <http://www.umm.edu/feature/ laughter

Sande, K. (2004) The Peacemaker: a bibilical guide to resolving personal conflict. Grand Rapids, MI: Baker Books

Twerrell, J.T. (1997). Marriage and Family Therapy an Integrated Approach. Sarasota, FL: NCCA

About the Author

Dr. Lea has more than thirty years of ministry experience. He holds the position of Congregational Care Pastor at Chesapeake Church in Huntingtown, Maryland. Dr. Lea provides oversight of the prayer ministry, the counseling ministries including pre-marital mentoring and married couples mentoring, and other care needs in the community. In this position Dr. Lea co-mentors with his wife couples who are planning to marry or are already married.

Dr. Lea is a Licensed Clinical Pastoral Counselor (NCCA), a National Certified Counselor (NBCC), a Licensed Clinical Professional Counselor, an ordained minister, and the author of Counseling Youth, NCCA and So You Think You Are Married ... Ten Tip On How To Live Like It, Westbow Press. As president of Calvert Christian Training Academy he assists others who are interested in becoming active in presenting the Gospel through the ministry of counseling.